# molly moon's

## HOMEMADE ICE CREAM

# molly moon's
## HOMEMADE ICE CREAM

*Sweet Seasonal Recipes for*
*Ice Creams, Sorbets & Toppings*
*Made with Local Ingredients*

*molly moon neitzel and christina spittler*

Printed in China

Published by Sasquatch Books
17 16 15 14 13 12          9 8 7 6 5 4 3 2 1

Cover photograph: Kathryn Barnard
Cover design: Gregory Flores
Interior photographs: Kathryn Barnard
Food styling: Callie Meyer and Patty Wittmann
Interior design: Gregory Flores
Interior composition: Sarah Plein
Carbon offsetting: Molly Moon's Homemade Ice Cream and Sustainable Energy Partners

Library of Congress Cataloging-in-Publication Data is available.

ISBN-13: 978-1-57061-810-9
ISBN-10: 1-57061-810-0

Sasquatch Books
1904 Third Avenue, Suite 710
Seattle, WA 98101
(206) 467-4300
www.sasquatchbooks.com
custserv@sasquatchbooks.com

# *for*
## my grandparents

*all of whom, in very much their own ways, shaped who I am and how I have hoped to contribute to the world. It was my Grandpa John's allowing me to have ice cream before lunch on so very many summer days that instilled in me a love of the cold, creamy treat, and a ritual of spoiling myself and those I love with sweet trips to the local ice cream shop. It was under the tutelage of my grandmothers, Angela and Faye, that I learned the arts of social responsibility and social grace that have pushed me forward in life, with my head held high. It is my Grandpa Herb's humor that keeps me light and gives me hope that life should be as fun as he seems to think!*

# contents

# ✢ recipe list

## winter

## always

# thank-yous

I couldn't have opened an ice cream shop or created the amazing community I have around my favorite treat without the love and support of Zack; my parents; my little sister, Anna; my grandparents; Charlie at the Big Dipper in Missoula; Debi; Andy and Deborah; and the kids at Music for America who taught me how to (and how not to) be a leader. And I couldn't keep it all going without Christina, Cindy, Jen, Kendal, and Sophia by my side. Special thanks to my mom and Zoe for reading this manuscript so many times. Thank you all so very much!

*molly moon neitzel*

Thank you to my parents, Marty and Tracy, for letting me waste countless amounts of groceries growing up as I created edible, and less than edible, concoctions in my quest to perfect my craft. For courageously eating, or pretending to eat, whatever I had most recently disguised as food, they, as well as my sisters, Brooke and Blair, are owed more thanks than I can sum up in this paragraph. Thank you to Angela and Patrick for holding down the kitchens in Wallingford and Capitol Hill, respectively, while I worked on this project; to Zoe for her recipe testing and editing; and to Molly for giving me the opportunity to contribute to this book. And thank you to Brian for his continued love and support.

*christina spittler*

Huge thanks go out from both of us to Shelley Bjornstad, our most enthusiastic recipe tester, and to the amazing Dirty Happy Girls: Kathryn Barnard and Callie Meyer. We couldn't have done this without you!

# introduction

I have always loved ice cream. I could eat it every day. And I probably have eaten ice cream almost every day of my life. When I was growing up, my mom always kept ice cream in the freezer for my dad, my little sister, and me. And my grandparents all knew it was my favorite treat. Ice cream sundaes were a big to-do at my Grandma Angie's house. She loved pulling out her special sundae dishes and the long spoons she saved just for extra-tall parfaits. She had bottles and jars of toppings in the fridge, and she always topped our creations with a cherry. I guess these ice cream affairs after family dinners had something to do with the way my grandmother met my grandfather, Herb, when he was a "soda jerk" in her neighborhood, the Chicago sub-urb of Oak Park. She would push her baby brother in a stroller up the street to the soda fountain and order a "double dip" on a cone. While Herb was scooping, she made sure he could see her jaunty little hat, on which she had embroidered her name, Angie, in pretty script. Once he had finished, and just before he handed her the cone, my grandma would scrunch up her nose and say, "Oh, I wanted the vanilla on top of the chocolate. Could you switch them?" just to keep him there a little longer!

In my late twenties, after years working in politics and the music industry and getting burned out on both, I desperately sought a new career that would satisfy my need for indepen-dence. It was then that I remembered my first love, ice cream, and I set out to create a place in Seattle where the Angies and Herbs of 2008 could meet.

You see, before a brief fundraising career, and before I was the executive director of a political nonprofit that worked with bands to politically engage their fans, I had a college job. And like most college girls, I sought work at a place where I could get my favorite thing for free. For me it wasn't a clothing boutique or a record store—it was an ice cream shop. From 1998 through 2000, I worked at the Big Dipper in Missoula, Montana, first as a scooper and later as an ice cream maker. In a few years, I learned most of what it takes to run an ice cream shop from an unorthodox col-lege mentor—Charlie, the Big Dipper's punk rock owner. I loved

# sustainable ice cream: what does that mean?

In creating our company, we committed ourselves to being an environmentally sustainable business. It is a philosophy that influences everything we do. Whether we are creating a new sundae with local fruits or nuts or using nontoxic cleaners to tidy up the shop after a busy day, we are always aware of our impact on the environment—locally and globally. This means doing our best to use local and organic ingredients whenever possible, as well as taking the seasons into full consideration when we create new toppings, ice creams, and sorbets.

## choosing between local and organic

In a perfect world, we would all be able to purchase organic foods grown by local farmers in our communities, all the time. Unfortunately, we know that it is just not that easy. With all the choices and variety available to consumers these days, taking a simple trip to the grocery store can become a perplexing and baffling experience. Do I buy the organic carrots from California? Or the nonorganic carrots from a nearby farming community? What about the hormone-free milk from a local dairy versus the organic milk from an out-of-state dairy? Are these organic raspberries available in January any better than the ones in the freezer case year-round? The truth is, there aren't easy answers to these questions, but taking some simple principles into consideration can dramatically help your decision-making process.

### local

Why is using local ingredients so important to us? There are several reasons. For one, the fewer miles your food has traveled to become your next meal, the fewer fossil fuels are burned. Whether your food travels by rail, ship, plane, or truck, it all requires some form of fuel to get from the farm to your kitchen. The shorter the distance, the smaller the amount of fossil fuels burned—and the smaller the amount of greenhouse gases, namely carbon dioxide, released into the atmosphere.

Eating locally also ensures that your food will taste better. Produce that must endure an arduous cross-country truck ride is often harvested prematurely to prevent bruising in transit. Choosing local foods that have not been harvested with shipping or packing as a priority means produce picked at the peak of freshness and, more importantly, ripeness. And ripe food means better flavor! Similarly, dairy that travels long distances between the cow and the kitchen means a more intense pasteurization process, which eliminates many of the healthy benefits of fresh milk and much of that fresh dairy taste.

Eating seasonally is a key component to eating locally and limiting the number of miles your food travels to get to you. To truly embrace the goods your local environment can offer, it is important to acknowledge that certain foods are available only during certain times of year. So does this mean we Northwesterners can enjoy the bounty of huckleberries only in the fall? Or that we are destined to enjoy a juicy peach solely during the fleeting month of August? No! Whether you freeze it, can it, jam it, pickle it, dehydrate it, smoke it, or cure it, any of the seasonal delights in your neck of the woods can be preserved using the time-tested techniques of the generations before us.

And of course, eating locally helps support your local economy. It is not news that farmers receive only a fraction of what you pay at the store for the food that they grow. The rest of that money pays for getting the food from the farm to your shopping cart in one piece. Fuel, truck maintenance, refrigeration, processing, and marketing are a few of these other expenses. When you buy foods grown locally, you are eliminating these additional costs, so more of the money you spend can go straight back to the farmers, contributing to the wellness of your entire community.

## organic

At Molly Moon's, we love to use organic ingredients in our ice creams and sorbets whenever possible. We believe that organic farming practices are the healthiest and most environmentally sustainable option and produce the tastiest food, and we want to pass that goodness on to our customers. Farming organically is a

better option than chemical-dependent farming, for a number of reasons. It promotes the development of healthy soils and water conservation because it does not make use of dangerous pesticides, herbicides, or synthetic fertilizers. Organic farmers use crop rotation techniques as well as beneficial insects to combat weeds and pests, and use natural fertilizers like manure and compost to help their crops grow. Avoiding chemically dependent farming methods not only keeps our bodies free from any lingering pesticide residues, but also keeps local watersheds free of harmful pollutants and keeps neighboring ecosystems intact.

Possibly the most important element of making the right food choices for your family or community is arming yourself with as much information as possible. Sometimes an organically certified product—using milk as an example—may come from cows raised on organically certified feed that was grown on other continents and required tons of fossil fuels to transport it to the dairy farm. At Molly Moon's, we are mindful that complicated food chains deserve careful attention.

## molly moon's american-style ice cream

There are two commonly used styles of ice cream base: Philadelphia, or "American" style and French "custard" style. Philadelphia-style ice cream usually consists of a combination of milk, cream, sugar, and any number of added flavorings such as vanilla, melted chocolate, lemon zest, and the like. Custard-style recipes call for nearly identical ingredients but include the addition of egg yolks. At Molly Moon's, we prefer to make Philadelphia-style ice cream, so the recipes in this book are all of that variety.

Our thinking is that by adding fewer elements to our ice cream bases, we are not only emphasizing the unadulterated, fresh, sweet cream taste of the local dairy we use, but also sourcing from one less animal, and using fewer resources to bring you the ice cream that you love.

However, French "custard" style ice cream is by no means inferior in taste or quality. In fact, many pastry chefs would argue it is the classic and traditional way to make ice cream. There are plenty of cookbooks out there that describe this method; our favorite is *The Perfect Scoop* by David Lebovitz.

# what you need to get started

We are so excited that you are about to start your ice cream–making journey! There are just a few common kitchen items you'll need to gather, an ice cream machine for you to choose, and a couple of quick tips to know. First, please realize that making ice cream is FUN! And you should treat it as such. These recipes should not intimidate you as much as, say, a baking cookbook might. Yes, you can mess up ice cream by scorching the milk, or not churning it long enough, or burning the caramel, but ice cream making is not rocket science. These recipes will be fun desserts to make by yourself or with a passel of kids helping you in the kitchen. And now for the tools and tips!

## notes for best results

When you churn ice cream or sorbet in your home machine, you are basically mixing in air while simultaneously freezing the water particles in the base. This creates a consistency that is lighter than the liquid you started with (because of the air) and more solid and stable (due to the freezing). It might sound complicated, but don't worry, your ice cream machine will take care of it. Here are a few things to remember to get the most out of these recipes and help you and your ice cream machine make the best frozen desserts possible.

### choosing a machine

There are several ice cream machines on the market to choose from, and they all pretty much do the same thing—churn air into your liquid ingredients while freezing them. The biggest question to answer in buying a machine is, "Do I want to make more than one batch in a twenty-four-hour period?" If the answer is yes, you will need a machine with a freezer component built into the unit. These are typically much more expensive machines, usually priced upward of $200. Our favorites are the Whynter 2-quart Ice Cream Maker and the Lello Musso Lussino 1.5-quart Ice Cream Maker. If you think you can live

### ice cream tools

- ice cream maker or churner
- heavy-bottomed, nonreactive saucepan
- liquid and dry measuring cups
- measuring spoons
- whisk
- flexible spatula, preferably silicone
- sharp knife
- shallow pan or bowl
- glass or plastic airtight food storage freezer containers in pint or quart sizes

### for added fun

- food mill or blender
- strainer or fine mesh sieve
- candy thermometer
- ice cream scoop
- cherry pitter
- electric stand mixer
- spice grinder or coffee grinder
- juicer
- citrus reamer
- grater
- kitchen scale
- parchment paper or a silicone baking mat
- pizzelle iron or cone baker for homemade waffle-style cones

## tips to remember

Read the recipe all the way through before you start! We promise, you'll be grateful.

Patience is really key when making ice creams and sorbets. To make a perfect frozen treat, you often need to wait a little longer than you want, to let the ingredients chill before putting them in the ice cream machine. Don't rush!

All ice cream makers are a little different and churn a different amount of air into the final product, so the number of servings you actually get will vary a bit.

Aluminum cookware that is unanodized—that is, not chemically treated—is not recommended for use in these recipes. Unanodized aluminum reacts with any even slightly acidic foods, like milk, cream, and most fruit, and the chemical reaction can taint the flavor and color of your final product. We recommend anodized aluminum and stainless steel cookware.

Your homemade ice cream will keep for about a week, depending on the consistency of your freezer's thermostat. But you can always make more!

# spring

honey lavender ice cream

carrot cake ice cream

salt licorice ice cream

"scout" mint ice cream

thai tea ice cream

blueberry goat's milk frozen yogurt

strawberry rhubarb sorbet

lavender lemonade sorbet

baby beet sorbet

lemon curd

cajeta

bee pollen sugar

rhubarb rose compote

# honey lavender ice cream

This recipe is truly fresh from the Northwest—specifically, the lush Olympic Peninsula. Roy at Tahuya River Apiaries (www.hiveharvest.com) has been beekeeping in the foothills of the Olympic Mountains for decades. He keeps us stocked with the most delicious Northwest wildflower honey and has since day one. You can find Roy or his son at many Seattle area farmers' markets. Just twenty miles away, nestled in the rain shadow of the Olympic Mountains, is Purple Haze Lavender (www.purplehazelavender.com) in Sequim, Washington. They supply our kitchens with fragrant, certified organic, dried lavender flowers year-round.

*MAKES 1 TO 1½ QUARTS*

2 cups heavy cream

1 cup whole milk

¼ cup sugar

¾ cup honey

1 tablespoon finely ground dried food-grade lavender flowers (see note)

Pinch of kosher salt

**NOTE**
*If your lavender comes as dried whole flowers, grind them into a fine powder in a spice grinder or well-cleaned coffee grinder. A mortar and pestle will work too, as will a sharp knife and some elbow grease.*

Put all the ingredients into a small, heavy-bottomed saucepan with a lid and cook, uncovered, over medium heat, whisking occasionally, until the sugar and honey are dissolved. Before the mixture comes to a boil, remove from the heat. Cover and let the mixture steep for 30 minutes.

Pour the mixture into a shallow pan or bowl and place in the refrigerator to chill thoroughly, 1 to 2 hours.

When the mixture is cold, pour it into an ice cream maker and process according to the manufacturer's instructions. Using a rubber spatula, transfer the ice cream to an airtight glass or plastic freezer container. Cover tightly and freeze until the ice cream is firm, at least 4 hours.

# carrot cake ice cream

Spring flavors can be tough in the Pacific Northwest, as our winter-to-spring transition can sometimes be a nail biter. June is the start of carrot season, and this flavor showcases them in their best form: carrot cake! No shortcuts were taken here, so we use real cream cheese, grated carrots, brown sugar, and spices in this recipe. It has proved to be a real hit with our customers, so we think you will love it. If you are a stickler for tradition, enjoy your scoop with a sprinkling of chopped walnuts or raisins!

*MAKES 1 TO 1½ QUARTS*

2 cups heavy cream

1 cup whole milk, divided

3/4 cup packed light brown sugar

Pinch of kosher salt

1½ cups finely grated carrot
    (about 3 medium carrots)

1 teaspoon ground cinnamon

1/4 teaspoon ground nutmeg

1/8 teaspoon ground cloves

4 ounces (1/2 cup) cream cheese,
    at room temperature

1 teaspoon vanilla extract

Put the cream, ¾ cup of the milk, and the brown sugar, salt, carrots, cinnamon, nutmeg, and cloves into a small, heavy-bottomed saucepan. Cook, uncovered, over medium heat, stirring occasionally to dissolve the sugar. Bring to a boil, then reduce the heat to low and let simmer gently for 20 minutes, stirring frequently to prevent scorching.

In a medium bowl, whisk the cream cheese and vanilla together until completely smooth. Gradually add the remaining ¼ cup milk, 1 tablespoon at a time, whisking vigorously until smooth after each addition. Pour the cream cheese into the carrot mixture and whisk until thoroughly combined. Pour the mixture into a shallow pan or bowl and refrigerate to chill thoroughly, 1 to 2 hours.

When the mixture is cold, pour it into an ice cream maker and process according to the manufacturer's instructions. Using a rubber spatula, transfer the ice cream to an airtight glass or plastic freezer container. Cover tightly and freeze until the ice cream is firm, at least 4 hours.

# salt licorice ice cream

When I worked my first ice cream job as a scooper at Goody's, an old-fashioned ice cream parlor and candy shop in Boise, Idaho, the older scoopers used to make the new hires chew on a piece of double-salt licorice as a kind of hazing ritual. When I bit into my first piece, I disappointed them all by exclaiming, "Mmmmmm! I *love* salty licorice!" Though it's a punishment to some, salt licorice is a much-anticipated flavor for many of our regular customers who share my affinity for this Danish-style treat. We release it every year on National Licorice Day, April 12, and keep it on the menu for a month or so. We like our Salt Licorice Ice Cream with a good bit of salt, but do not hesitate to adjust this recipe to your own personal taste.

*MAKES 1 TO 1½ QUARTS*

2 cups heavy cream

1 cup whole milk

¾ cup sugar

1 tablespoon kosher salt

15 whole star anise pods (see note)

1 tablespoon ouzo or other anise-flavored liqueur

### NOTE
*When buying star anise, look for pods with as few broken pieces as possible. The pod itself, not the seeds inside, is where the licorice flavor resides, so resist any temptation to break or crush the pods.*

Put the cream, milk, sugar, salt, and star anise into a small, heavy-bottomed saucepan with a lid. Cook over medium heat, whisking occasionally to dissolve the sugar. When the mixture begins to simmer gently, remove from the heat. Cover and let the mixture steep at room temperature for 1 hour. Transfer the mixture to a shallow pan or bowl and place in the refrigerator to chill thoroughly, 1 to 2 hours.

When the mixture is cold, strain it through a fine mesh sieve. Discard the sieve contents. Whisk the liqueur into the mixture. Pour it into an ice cream maker and process according to the manufacturer's instructions. Using a rubber spatula, transfer the ice cream to an airtight glass or plastic freezer container. Cover tightly and freeze until the ice cream is firm, at least 4 hours.

# "scout" mint ice cream

This ice cream is the embodiment of one of my very favorite community aspects about Molly Moon's. I learned more of my business skills than I should probably admit as a Girl Scout selling cookies all over town. The "camperships" offered to the girls who sold a lot of cookies played an important role in the affordability of Girl Scout camp for me. Camp was one of the very best parts of my childhood and ended up shaping who I am in many ways. As a grown-up, I find it amazingly fun to be able to support little Scouts now by buying tens of thousands of cookies every spring. We buy enough Thin Mints during cookie season to supply all of our shops with an entire year's worth of cookies for one of our most popular flavors. These purchases often shock the girls, who get bigger sales if I think their pitch is particularly good (teaching those business skills early!). Last spring, when I bought 325 boxes of cookies from one articulate little lady, her mom started crying—our purchase had just gotten her a full ride to camp! "Scout" Mint is sure to be a crowd pleaser—especially with the under-ten-years-old set!

## MAKES 1 TO 1½ QUARTS

1 cup whole milk

2 cups heavy cream

¾ cup sugar

Pinch of kosher salt

2 teaspoons peppermint extract

1½ cups crushed Thin Mint Girl Scout cookies (about 15 cookies) (see note)

### NOTE
*The cookies can be crushed into pieces as big or small as you want them to be in your ice cream. We shoot for pea-size pieces and leave a cookie or two mostly intact—because who doesn't love finding a big cookie in their ice cream?*

Put the milk, cream, sugar, and salt into a small, heavy-bottomed saucepan. Cook over medium heat, whisking occasionally to dissolve the sugar. Before the mixture has come to a boil, remove from the heat. Pour the mixture into a shallow pan or bowl and place in the refrigerator to chill thoroughly, 1 to 2 hours.

When the mixture is cold, stir in the peppermint extract. Pour it into an ice cream maker and process according to the manufacturer's instructions. During the last few minutes of processing, add the cookies. Using a rubber spatula, transfer the ice cream to an airtight glass or plastic freezer container. Cover tightly and freeze until the ice cream is firm, at least 4 hours.

# thai tea ice cream

This ice cream is rich and exotic tasting while still being light. Something about this taste gives me a satisfaction similar to good dark chocolate. I love a sweet Thai iced tea with my Pad See Ew, and now I can make the perfect dessert to pair with my amateur homemade version! Note: Try and get your hands on organic and fair trade Rooibos and Assam tea leaves that are not scented or combined with other types of tea or flavorings. Good-quality, bulk loose leaf tea is available in the coffee and tea section of some grocery stores, but if you are having trouble finding some, check out www.mountainroseherbs.com to get just what you need.

*MAKES A SCANT 1 QUART*

2 cups heavy cream

1 cup whole milk

1 cup sugar

Pinch of kosher salt

1 cup red tea leaves, such as Rooibos

2 tablespoons black tea leaves, such as Assam

1 cinnamon stick

1/2 teaspoon anise seeds

1 teaspoon vanilla extract

Put the cream, milk, sugar, salt, tea leaves, cinnamon, and anise into a small, heavy-bottomed saucepan with a lid. Cook, uncovered, over medium heat, whisking occasionally, until the sugar is dissolved. Bring the mixture to a simmer, then remove from the heat and cover. Let steep for 30 minutes at room temperature. After 30 minutes, pour the mixture through a fine mesh sieve and press down firmly with a spatula or the back of a ladle to squeeze out any remaining liquid. Discard the sieve contents. Pour the reserved mixture into a shallow pan or bowl and place in the refrigerator to chill thoroughly, 1 to 2 hours.

When the mixture is cold, whisk in the vanilla. Pour into an ice cream maker and process according to the manufacturer's instructions. Using a rubber spatula, transfer the ice cream to an airtight glass or plastic freezer container. Cover tightly and freeze until the ice cream is firm, at least 4 hours.

# blueberry goat's milk frozen yogurt

Tim and Grace Lukens of Grace Harbor Farms supply us with goat's milk yogurt fresh from their farm in Custer, Washington, about a hundred miles north of Seattle. Swirled with sweet blueberry compote, this frozen yogurt is such a refreshing treat, and it's a great option for Molly Moon's fans who must avoid cow's milk products. You are sure to gain a following when you share this unique flavor with friends and family. Be sure to cool the compote completely before adding it to the frozen yogurt . . . otherwise you could end up with yogurt soup!

*MAKES 1 TO 1½ QUARTS*

**For the blueberry compote:**

2 cups fresh or frozen blueberries

¾ cup sugar

2 tablespoons freshly
    squeezed lemon juice

**For the frozen yogurt:**

2½ cups goat's milk yogurt

½ cup sugar

½ cup honey

1 tablespoon vanilla extract

To make the compote, put the blueberries, sugar, and lemon juice into a small, nonreactive saucepan. Bring to a simmer over medium-low heat and cook, stirring occasionally, until thick, 10 to 15 minutes. Remove from the heat and pour the compote into a shallow pan or bowl. Place in the refrigerator to chill completely, about 1 hour.

To make the frozen yogurt, in a large bowl combine the yogurt, sugar, honey, and vanilla. Whisk until the sugar and honey are completely dissolved. Place in the refrigerator to chill thoroughly, about 1 hour.

When the yogurt mixture is cold, pour it into an ice cream maker and process according to the manufacturer's instructions. Remove the blueberry compote from the refrigerator. Using a rubber spatula, transfer one quarter of the frozen yogurt to an airtight glass or plastic freezer container and top with one third of the compote. Repeat until all of the yogurt and compote are layered. Cover tightly and freeze until the frozen yogurt is firm, at least 4 hours.

# strawberry rhubarb sorbet

You know it's spring in the Pacific Northwest when fresh, bright red and green rhubarb is everywhere at the farmers' markets. The combination of strawberries and rhubarb gives this sorbet the perfect texture. It is smooth, creamy, and the kind of tangy-sweet that makes your cheeks pucker before you dig in for another bite!

*MAKES 1 TO 1½ QUARTS*

2 cups water, divided

5 stalks rhubarb, coarsely chopped (about 3 cups)

3/4 cup coarsely chopped fresh or frozen strawberries (fresh berries should be rinsed and hulled)

2 cups sugar

2 tablespoons freshly squeezed lemon juice

Pour 1 cup of the water into a small, nonreactive saucepan. Bring to a simmer over low heat and add the rhubarb. Gently cook the rhubarb over low heat until it is tender and the pieces are falling apart, 10 to 12 minutes. If the mixture starts to dry out, add more water, ¼ cup at a time. Pour the cooked rhubarb and the strawberries into a blender and purée thoroughly. Measure out 2¼ cups of the strawberry-rhubarb purée. If your purée falls short, add enough water to make 2¼ cups. Pour it into a shallow bowl and refrigerate until completely chilled, 1 to 2 hours.

While the purée is cooling, bring the remaining 1 cup water and the sugar just to a boil over high heat, whisking to dissolve the sugar. Remove the sugar syrup from the heat and pour into a shallow bowl. Place in the refrigerator to chill thoroughly, about 1 hour.

When both the purée and the syrup are thoroughly chilled, combine them and add the lemon juice. Pour the mixture into an ice cream maker and process according to the manufacturer's instructions. Using a rubber spatula, transfer the sorbet to an airtight glass or plastic freezer container. Cover tightly and freeze until the sorbet is firm, at least 4 hours.

# lavender lemonade sorbet

This sorbet wins the award for prettiest color in my book. I've seen it vary from a light purplish pink to a dark fuchsia hue, depending on how finely the lavender is ground and how long it is steeped. In our constant search to come up with the next tasty and exciting ice cream or sorbet flavor, we occasionally refer to our customer suggestion inbox, and that is where we found this flavor combination. Do you have a creative flavor idea that can be locally sourced and is delicious? Submit it on our website today!

*MAKES 1 TO 1½ QUARTS*

2 cups sugar

2½ cups water

2 tablespoons ground dried
food-grade lavender flowers
(see note on page 2)

¾ cup freshly squeezed
lemon juice (from about
4 large lemons)

Put the sugar and water into a small, heavy-bottomed saucepan with a lid. Over high heat, bring just to a boil, whisking to dissolve the sugar. Remove from the heat and whisk in the lavender. Cover and let the mixture steep for 20 minutes at room temperature. After 20 minutes, whisk in the lemon juice. Pour the mixture into a shallow pan or bowl and place in the refrigerator to chill thoroughly, 1 to 2 hours.

Pour the mixture into an ice cream maker and process according to the manufacturer's instructions. Using a rubber spatula, transfer the sorbet to an airtight glass or plastic freezer container. Cover tightly and freeze until the sorbet is firm, at least 4 hours.

## compotes of everything!

At Molly Moon's, we make delicious compotes out of almost anything we can get our hands on. Our very first shop opened with a strawberry-rhubarb compote on the menu that really set the bar high. Our seasonal compotes are now one of the things customers look forward to coming in to try. Some of our favorite Northwest ingredients to use in compotes include apples, blueberries, cranberries, huckleberries, peaches, pears, blackberries, and strawberries.

A basic recipe for compote follows. Remember that all fruit is different and should be tasted for sweetness. Feel free to adjust the amount of sugar based on your fruit.

2 cups fruit, fresh or frozen

3/4 cup sugar

2 tablespoons freshly squeezed lemon juice

Put all the ingredients into a small, nonreactive saucepan. Over medium-low heat, bring to a simmer and cook, stirring occasionally, until thick, 10 to 15 minutes. For a thicker compote, cook for 5 to 8 minutes more. Serve warm or chilled.

# baby beet sorbet

This sorbet was a product of one of our very early spring creative meetings. We were tired of winter, craving spring ingredients, but it just wasn't warm enough for rhubarb or berries or cherries. One of our ice cream makers, a young, aspiring locavore chef named Nick, had seen baby beets at the market and came up with this flavor. We created a sundae around it called "Sweet Dirt," topping this intensely hued sorbet with shaved carrots, balsamic vinegar reduction, and grated Parmesan. It was a total hit!

*MAKES 1 TO 1½ QUARTS*

12 ounces baby beets (12 to 14 beets), unpeeled, washed and quartered, ends trimmed

2 cups sugar

1 cup water

2 tablespoons freshly squeezed lemon juice

Place the beets in a small, heavy-bottomed saucepan and add water to cover by an inch. Bring to a boil over high heat. Reduce the heat to low and let simmer, uncovered, until the beets are thoroughly cooked and tender all the way through, 25 to 30 minutes. Test their doneness by inserting a fork into the thickest beet. If it slides in and out without resistance, your beets are done; if not, continue to cook. If necessary, add enough water to keep the beets partially submerged while cooking. When done, remove from the heat, pour the beets and cooking liquid into a blender, and purée thoroughly. You should have 2 cups (16 fluid ounces) of beet purée. If your purée falls short, add water to yield 2 cups. Pour it into a shallow bowl or pan and place in the refrigerator to chill thoroughly, about 1 hour.

While the purée is chilling, bring the sugar and water just to a boil in a small saucepan over high heat, whisking to dissolve the sugar. Pour the sugar syrup into a shallow pan or bowl and place in the refrigerator to chill thoroughly, about 1 hour.

When the beet purée and sugar syrup are thoroughly chilled, combine them and whisk in the lemon juice. Pour the mixture into an ice cream maker and process according to the manufacturer's instructions. Using a rubber spatula, transfer the sorbet to an airtight glass or plastic freezer container. Cover tightly and freeze until the sorbet is firm, at least 4 hours.

# lemon curd

I find lemon curd really rewarding to make. I have zero formal dessert or pastry training, but I can easily make a perfect batch of lemon curd if I just pay attention. It always comes out feeling like a feat and impresses anyone with its rich and intense flavor. It just feels fancy to me! Lemon curd is the ideal topping for honey lavender ice cream, but I also love it on toast.

*MAKES ABOUT 4 CUPS*

8 large eggs

4 large egg yolks

2 cups sugar

1½ cups freshly squeezed lemon juice (from about 8 large lemons)

Pinch of kosher salt

½ cup (1 stick) unsalted butter, at room temperature

¼ cup heavy cream

1 teaspoon vanilla extract

Set up a double boiler by placing a large pot filled with 2 inches of water over medium-low heat. In a glass or metal bowl that rests securely on the top of the pot without touching the water, whisk together the eggs, yolks, and sugar. Bring the water to a simmer and set the bowl over the pot. Gradually whisk the lemon juice and salt into the egg and sugar mixture. Keeping the water at a simmer, allow the curd to cook on the double boiler until thick, 12 to 15 minutes, whisking and scraping the sides of the bowl occasionally. When the curd is noticeably thicker, carefully remove the bowl from the pot.

While the curd is still warm, whisk in the butter, cream, and vanilla. Strain through a fine mesh sieve to remove any overcooked egg particles or shell. Discard the sieve contents. Transfer to a shallow storage container and place plastic wrap directly on the surface of the curd to prevent a skin from forming. Place in the refrigerator to chill thoroughly, about 2 hours. Lemon curd will keep in the fridge for about 4 days.

# cajeta

Cajeta is a caramel made by slowly cooking and caramelizing sweetened goat's or cow's milk. It is a common confection in Central and South America, especially popular in Mexico, and it is truly delicious drizzled atop melted chocolate ice cream. Spring is the season for local goat's milk in the Pacific Northwest. The most important ingredient in this recipe is patience! Do not rush this one, or your cajeta will foam over and you will have a sticky mess on your stovetop.

*MAKES ABOUT 2½ CUPS*

4 cups goat's milk

2 cups sugar

¼ cup honey

¼ teaspoon baking soda

Pinch of kosher salt

Put all the ingredients in a medium, heavy-bottomed saucepan and whisk over medium heat to dissolve the sugar and honey. Carefully bring to a boil and then reduce the heat to low. Adjusting the heat as needed, keep the cajeta at a simmer until the color changes to a dark brown and the mixture reaches 225°F on a candy thermometer, about 45 minutes. Keep an eye on the mixture throughout, as it can easily boil over if left unattended, but stir infrequently—it tends to foam over the more it is stirred.

When it reaches 225°F, remove from the heat and let cool at room temperature; it will thicken as it cools. Store in an airtight container in the refrigerator for up to 1 month. Cajeta can be served warm, cold, or at room temperature.

# bee pollen sugar

This topping started out as an experiment for our "April Showers" sundae. We wanted a pretty sprinkle of something to top honey lavender ice cream, lemon curd, and fresh whipped cream. This mixture became one of our favorites. It is also great on top of yogurt, oatmeal, and smoothies. You can buy bee pollen granules at most health food stores and at some smoothie shops. Be aware that some people are allergic to bee pollen, so make sure you know your audience if you are serving this to guests.

*MAKES ABOUT 1½ CUPS*

½ cup bee pollen granules

½ cup clear crystal sugar, clear sanding sugar, or demerara sugar

¼ cup dried food-grade lavender flowers, whole

½ cup dried food-grade rose petals (optional)

Combine and thoroughly mix all the ingredients together. Stored in an airtight container in a dry place, bee pollen sugar can keep for about 1 month.

# rhubarb rose compote

We love rose! Rose water is one of our secret weapons in the kitchen. However, please note: it should be used with caution, as a little goes a long way. You would be surprised at how easy it is to make your favorite dessert taste like your grandmother's perfume. In this recipe, its subtle floral flavor really complements the sweet and tangy bite of the rhubarb. This compote was first featured on our menu in April 2009 for the opening of our Capitol Hill shop. Pair this with some vanilla bean ice cream and Crispy Nut Cobbler-Top Crumble (page 50). Yum!

*MAKES ABOUT 2 CUPS*

3½ cups coarsely chopped rhubarb (about 6 stalks)

1 cup sugar

1 tablespoon freshly squeezed lemon juice

2 tablespoons rose water

Combine the rhubarb, sugar, and lemon juice in a medium nonreactive saucepan. Cook over medium-low heat, stirring occasionally with a wooden spoon, until the rhubarb begins to break down and fall apart, 10 to 12 minutes. Remove from the heat and stir in the rose water. Serve hot or cold. Store in an airtight container in the refrigerator for up to 2 weeks.

how to make . . .

# . . . an ice cream cake

## Here are some tips and tricks for making your very own ice cream cake at home:

Pick a cake that you like. Bake it. Cool it. Freeze it. You can pretty much turn any cake into an ice cream cake. If you don't believe me, give it a shot! The worst that can happen is that you end up with cake and ice cream. The only rule is that you should bake your cake in basic round baking pans or in a springform pan. You could go with a square or rectangle shape, but any baker will tell you that those corners can be tricky to frost. Wrapped well in plastic wrap, many cakes can store in the freezer for at least a week or two. Freezing the cake before assembly makes it easier to cut and helps keep the ice cream from melting as quickly.

Cut the cake into layers. How many layers will it be? Two? Three? If you are ambitious, go for four! When cutting the cake into layers, be sure it's mostly frozen, and use a serrated knife. Making a shallow initial cut in the cake as a guide before you cut all the way through will ensure even layers. Inserting toothpicks as guides at intervals along that cut line is essential for beginners. Keep the cake layers frozen until you need them.

Make some ice cream. Be sure to pick a flavor that will complement your cake well and vice versa. Some of our favorite combos are chocolate cake with "Scout" Mint or Cappuccino Ice Cream, and vanilla cake with Strawberry Ice Cream. Whatever flavor of ice cream you decide to make, just be sure you make it on the same day that you want to assemble the cake. Making an ice cream cake with ice cream fresh out of the machine is ideal for easy spreadability. The quantity of ice cream needed will depend on how big your cake is and how many layers you want to make.

Assemble your cake. This part can be intimidating for beginners, but just relax and have fun! To start, make sure you have plenty of space cleared in your freezer for easy storage. Keep everything you are not using frozen. Dividing the ice cream evenly based on how many layers you are planning to fill is a great way to ensure even layers. For example, if you have three layers of cake, that means two layers of ice cream, so you would split the ice cream in half evenly. Start with one layer of cake and dollop its portion of ice cream on top, smoothing it out with a knife or, better yet, an offset spatula. Put this first layer in the freezer. Repeat this process with the other layers (except the top layer, of course). Once all of your lower cake layers have an even layer of ice cream on top, stack the layers and freeze immediately. The cake will need to set up in the freezer for at least 4 hours.

Leave the cake naked or feel free to frost the sides and top with freshly whipped cream, buttercream frosting, or more ice cream. Store it in the freezer until you are ready to serve. You did it! Now enjoy!

# summer

ginger ice cream

strawberry ice cream

cherry chocolate chunk ice cream

blackberry sage ice cream

peach sorbet

raspberry mint sorbet

tomato basil sorbet

cucumber mint sorbet

watermelon sorbet

cold chocolate sauce

raspberry coulis

butterscotch sauce

grilled stone fruit

crispy nut cobbler-top crumble

You can turn almost any ice cream into a more complex dessert by adding a ribbon through it. The most popular instance of this at Molly Moon's shops is our balsamic strawberry ice cream. When I was growing up, my mom made an amazing salad with baby spinach, strawberries, and a tangy balsamic vinaigrette. It was one of my favorites, and I really wanted to replicate the flavors in an ice cream. We use organic honey balsamic vinegar from the Pacific Northwest, but you can use any balsamic vinegar you would like!

## *balsamic reduction*

*MAKES ABOUT 1 CUP*

2 cups balsamic vinegar

2/3 cup sugar

Place a ceramic plate in the freezer to chill for testing the consistency of the reduction. Whisk the vinegar and sugar together in a small, heavy-bottomed, nonreactive saucepan. Set over medium heat and bring to a boil. Reduce the heat to low and let simmer until the mixture has reduced by half or reaches 230°F on a candy thermometer, 10 to 15 minutes. To test the consistency, spoon a couple of drops of reduction onto the chilled plate and hold the plate vertically. If the drops run rapidly down the plate, the reduction is too thin and needs to cook more. If the drops run slowly down the plate, the reduction is ready. Transfer the reduction to a shallow container and set aside. Cool to room temperature before use.

To assemble, make strawberry ice cream as instructed, but layer the room-temperature reduction into the processed ice cream as you transfer it from the ice cream maker to the container.

# ice cream sandwiches

The Earl of Sandwich was on to something when he slapped that bread around a hunk of meat oh so long ago. What better way to enjoy a scoop of ice cream than squished between two tasty cookies? Ice cream sandwiches are simple to make on your own, but you should follow these tips for Molly Moon–caliber treats:

- Choose the right cookie: A good ice cream sandwich needs a foolproof cookie. For easy handling and munching, we suggest a more flat than domed style of cookie. To achieve this, you can halve the quantity of baking soda and baking powder in your favorite cookie recipe. Using cookie dough that is at room temperature, rather than frozen or straight out of the refrigerator, will also make for a flatter cookie. Also, a greased sheet pan will help the cookie dough spread while baking.

- Underbake to perfection: For a perfect ice cream sandwich, it is imperative to underbake your cookie ever so slightly. Keeping the cookie on the chewier side of things ensures texture perfection after the whole shebang has set up in the freezer for a couple of hours.

- Keep your cookies cold: After you have baked and cooled your cookies, get them into a heavy-duty plastic bag and into the freezer for at least an hour. This will help keep the ice cream from melting prematurely when you assemble your sandies.

- Do your wrists a favor: When the time has come to put that scoop of ice cream between your lovely frozen cookies, help yourself out by using ice cream that either (1) you have just recently made and is setting up in the freezer, or (2) has been in the refrigerator softening for 20 to 30 minutes. Not only will the ice cream be easier to scoop, it will conform to the desired shape much more readily.

# gingerbread and cinnamon
# ice cream sandwiches

*MAKES 10 TO 12 ICE CREAM
SANDWICHES*

1½ cups all-purpose flour

½ teaspoon baking soda

½ teaspoon kosher salt

2 teaspoons ground ginger

1 teaspoon ground cinnamon

½ teaspoon ground allspice

¼ teaspoon ground cloves

½ cup (1 stick) unsalted
butter, softened

¼ cup granulated sugar

¼ cup packed dark brown sugar

¼ cup molasses

2 large egg yolks

½ cup finely chopped crystallized
ginger (optional)

1 batch Cinnamon Ice Cream (page
56), made fresh and almost set,
or softened in the refrigerator
for 20 to 30 minutes

Now that you know the tricks of making ice cream sandwiches, here is one of our favorite recipes for you to try.

Preheat the oven to 350°F. Line 2 baking sheets with parchment paper and set aside. In a small bowl, whisk together the flour, baking soda, salt, ginger, cinnamon, allspice, and cloves. Set aside. In another bowl, cream the butter, sugars, and molasses until light and fluffy. Beat in the egg yolks one at a time, scraping down the sides of the bowl after each addition. Beat until smooth. Carefully fold the flour mixture and the crystallized ginger into the butter mixture. Cover with plastic wrap and let the dough sit at room temperature for 30 minutes.

Pinch off pieces of dough and roll into balls about 1 inch in diameter. Evenly space the dough balls on the prepared cookie sheets. Cover the dough balls on one baking sheet with a piece of parchment paper or a silicone baking mat (slick side down). Using another cookie sheet or a cutting board, gently press down on the dough balls to slightly flatten them and create small disks. Carefully remove the parchment paper or silicone mat and repeat with the remaining dough balls on the other baking sheet. Bake for 4 to 5 minutes, rotate the cookie sheet, and bake until the cookies' surface appears slightly puffed but the edges have not browned at all, 2 to 3 minutes more. Remove from the oven and cool completely on the baking sheets. When completely cooled, transfer the cookies to a heavy plastic bag and place in the freezer for at least 30 minutes to chill.

To assemble the sandwiches, arrange half of the frozen cookies on a cookie sheet, top side down. Using a round scoop, dish a 2- or 3-ounce scoop (¼ to ⅓ cup) of softened cinnamon ice cream onto each cookie. Working quickly, top each scoop with another cookie, top side up, and press down gently. Immediately place in the freezer and allow the ice cream sandwiches to set for 2 hours before eating. Ice cream sandwiches can be stored in an airtight container or securely wrapped in plastic wrap in the freezer for up to 2 weeks.

# blackberry sage ice cream

Blackberry bushes are perhaps the most profuse plant in the Pacific Northwest, which makes a blackberry ice cream an absolute necessity in our shops. I get a little tired of blackberry fever—that time each August when every restaurant menu and farmers' market has blackberry items—so I decided to punch up our blackberry offering with an herbaceous twist. I love this flavor combination alongside a slice of pound cake.

*MAKES 1 TO 1½ QUARTS*

3 cups fresh or frozen blackberries

1½ cups sugar, divided

¼ cup freshly squeezed lemon juice (from about 2 lemons)

2 cups heavy cream

1 cup whole milk

10 fresh sage leaves, finely minced (about 1½ tablespoons)

1 teaspoon vanilla extract

Put the blackberries, 1 cup of the sugar, and the lemon juice into a small, nonreactive saucepan. Place over medium heat and cook, stirring occasionally, until thick, 10 to 13 minutes. Divide the blackberry mixture in half by pouring it into two separate bowls. Strain one half of the blackberries through a fine mesh sieve. Discard the sieve contents. Pour the strained blackberries into a shallow pan or bowl and combine with the unstrained blackberries. Place in the refrigerator to chill completely, 45 minutes to 1 hour.

While the blackberries are cooling, put the cream, milk, remaining ½ cup sugar, and sage into another small saucepan with a lid and cook over medium heat, uncovered, whisking to dissolve the sugar. Bring the cream mixture just to a boil and then remove from the heat. Cover and let steep for 20 minutes at room temperature. Pour the cream mixture into a shallow pan or bowl and place in the refrigerator to chill thoroughly, 1 to 2 hours.

When the blackberries and the cream mixture are both thoroughly chilled, whisk them together in a large bowl, then add the vanilla. Pour into an ice cream maker and process according to the manufacturer's instructions. Using a rubber spatula, transfer the ice cream to an airtight glass or plastic freezer container. Cover tightly and freeze until the ice cream is firm, at least 4 hours.

# make a shake!

Making a milkshake out of your homemade or store-bought ice cream is super easy. Simply put three large scoops (about 5 ounces each) of ice cream into your blender, and pour milk over the top until it reaches half the height of the ice cream. Blend until thoroughly combined. Serve immediately! Fun fact: A traditional old-fashioned chocolate milkshake is actually made with three scoops of vanilla ice cream, hot fudge or cold chocolate sauce, and milk—not with chocolate ice cream. Use as much hot fudge or chocolate sauce as you like to make your shake as chocolately as you prefer.

# peach sorbet

We love our local fruit purveyor, Remlinger Farms. They grow tasty strawberries, raspberries, peaches, and apples. Their peaches are bursting with tangy peach flavor, but this year, we were feeling like the peach sorbet needed a little more intense peach flavor and a slightly smoother texture, so we found a fun secret ingredient: peach schnapps! Don't worry—you won't get tipsy. (Unless you sip from the bottle while you work!)

*MAKES 1 TO 1½ QUARTS*

2 cups sugar

1 cup water

2 large or 3 small peaches, peeled, pitted, and quartered

2 tablespoons freshly squeezed lemon juice

1 tablespoon peach schnapps or peach-flavored liqueur

Combine the sugar and water in a small, stainless steel pot. Cook over medium heat, whisking occasionally, until the sugar has dissolved. Remove from the heat and set aside. Meanwhile, put the peaches in a blender with the lemon juice and purée thoroughly, 30 to 45 seconds. Pour the peach purée into a large bowl and whisk in the reserved sugar syrup. Transfer to a shallow pan or bowl and place in the refrigerator to chill completely, 1 to 2 hours.

When the mixture is thoroughly chilled, whisk in the schnapps. Pour the mixture into an ice cream maker and process according to the manufacturer's instructions. Using a rubber spatula, transfer the sorbet to an airtight glass or plastic freezer container. Cover tightly and freeze until the sorbet is firm, at least 4 hours.

# raspberry mint sorbet

The first time I tasted fresh mint with ripe summer fruit, I just about died from flavor explosion happiness. It is one of my very favorite parts of summer, and the most common breakfast in our house in July and August. Raspberry mint sorbet is a little taste of summer that can easily be made year-round with frozen raspberries and greenhouse mint. I try to pick twice as many berries as I think I'll need, then freeze half, so I can get this summer taste during the January doldrums!

*MAKES 1 TO 1½ QUARTS*

1 cup water

2 cups sugar

½ cup finely chopped spearmint leaves, divided

3 cups fresh or frozen raspberries (if using frozen, make sure they are completely thawed before using)

¼ cup freshly squeezed lemon juice (from about 2 lemons)

Put the water, sugar, and all but 2 tablespoons of the mint into a small, heavy-bottomed saucepan with a lid. Cook over medium heat, whisking occasionally, until the sugar is dissolved. Before the mixture comes to a boil, remove from the heat. Cover and let the mixture steep for 30 minutes at room temperature. Pour the mint syrup into a shallow bowl and refrigerate until completely chilled, about 1 hour.

Meanwhile, thoroughly purée the raspberries with the lemon juice in a blender, 30 to 45 seconds.

Evenly divide the purée between two bowls. Strain one half of the purée through a fine mesh sieve. Discard the sieve contents. Combine the strained and unstrained purées and place in the refrigerator to chill.

When the mint syrup is thoroughly chilled, strain it through a fine mesh sieve. Discard the sieve contents. In a medium bowl, combine the strained mint syrup and the raspberry purée.

Pour the mixture into an ice cream maker and process according to the manufacturer's instructions. Sprinkle the reserved 2 tablespoons mint leaves into the machine during the last minute of processing. Using a rubber spatula, transfer the sorbet to an airtight glass or plastic freezer container. Cover tightly and freeze until the sorbet is firm, at least 4 hours.

# tomato basil sorbet

A ripe tomato in season is truly a beautiful thing. This recipe works well with all tomatoes, but our favorites are organic heirloom varieties from Billy's Gardens in Tonasket, Washington—they are truly the best. We like to keep the skins on for more texture and flavor, but if you like a smoother consistency, strain the tomato and lemon juice mixture after blending it and before combining with the basil syrup.

*MAKES 1 TO 1½ QUARTS*

2 cups sugar

1 cup water

¼ cup finely chopped basil leaves

4 medium tomatoes, cored and quartered

2 tablespoons freshly squeezed lemon juice

Put the sugar, water, and basil into a small, nonreactive saucepan with a lid. Over medium heat, bring the mixture just to a boil, whisking to dissolve the sugar. Remove from the heat, cover, and let steep for 30 minutes at room temperature.

Put the tomatoes and lemon juice into a blender and purée thoroughly, 30 to 45 seconds. Pour the tomato purée into a large bowl and whisk in the chilled basil syrup. Pour the mixture into a shallow pan or bowl and place in the refrigerator to chill thoroughly, 1 to 2 hours.

When the mixture is cold, pour it into an ice cream maker and process according to the manufacturer's instructions. Using a rubber spatula, transfer the sorbet to an airtight glass or plastic freezer container. Cover tightly and freeze until the sorbet is firm, at least 4 hours.

# cucumber mint sorbet

This sorbet is a favorite of Christina's. She *loves* cucumbers! And what better way to eat your vegetables than in a refreshing sorbet? Cucumbers do very well in Eastern Washington, where it is hot and dry in the summer months. We use organic cucumbers from Inaba Farms in Wapato, Washington, and from Tonnemaker Family Orchard in Royal City, Washington. We like to use the basic garden cucumber because that bright green skin makes a beautiful emerald-colored sorbet. Try to avoid using cucumbers that have a waxed skin, and if the green color isn't appetizing to you, peel your cukes for a different look.

*MAKES 1 TO 1½ QUARTS*

1 cup water

1¾ cups sugar

2 cups cucumber juice (from about 2 medium cucumbers; see note), chilled

2 tablespoons freshly squeezed lemon juice

¼ cup finely chopped spearmint leaves

**NOTE**

*If you don't have access to a juicer, you can thoroughly purée 3 or 4 coarsely chopped cucumbers in a blender and strain through a fine mesh sieve to yield 2 cups liquid. Discard the sieve contents.*

Put the water and sugar into a small, heavy-bottomed saucepan. Over medium heat, bring just to a boil, whisking to dissolve the sugar. Pour the syrup into a shallow pan or bowl and refrigerate until chilled thoroughly, 1 to 2 hours.

When the sugar syrup is cold, whisk in the cucumber and lemon juices. Pour the mixture into an ice cream maker and process according to the manufacturer's instructions. During the last minute of processing, add the mint. Using a rubber spatula, transfer the sorbet to an airtight glass or plastic freezer container. Cover tightly and freeze until the sorbet is firm, at least 4 hours.

# watermelon sorbet

We have made cantaloupe mint sorbet a few times, but last year we tried watermelon sorbet, and this melon flavor knocked it out of the park! Create a homemade Bellini by pouring a bit of champagne or sparkling wine over a mini-scoop of this sorbet.

*MAKES 1 TO 1½ QUARTS*

2 cups sugar

1½ cups water

1½ pounds seedless watermelon, cut into 1-inch chunks

2 tablespoons freshly squeezed lemon juice

Put the sugar and water into a small, heavy-bottomed saucepan. Over medium heat, bring just to a boil, whisking to dissolve the sugar. Pour the mixture into a shallow pan or bowl and place in the refrigerator to chill thoroughly, 1 to 2 hours.

Meanwhile, purée the watermelon thoroughly in a blender. Place in the refrigerator until completely chilled, about 1 hour.

When the sugar syrup is cold, whisk in the lemon juice and the watermelon purée. Pour the mixture into an ice cream maker and process according to the manufacturer's instructions. Using a rubber spatula, transfer the sorbet to an airtight glass or plastic freezer container. Cover tightly and freeze until the sorbet is firm, at least 4 hours.

## turn anything into a mollypop!

When you make a list of fun things to do with homemade ice creams and sorbets, don't forget frozen pops (or MollyPops, as we call them)—the stuff of sweet childhood memories! Any of our recipes can be poured into frozen pop (or ice pop) molds, instead of going into the ice cream maker, to create sweet treats on sticks. We love any sorbet turned into a pop, as well as chocolate ice cream for fudge-pops. If you want to get really fancy, make two kinds of sorbet and layer them, or layer a sorbet and a vanilla ice cream for the Creamsicle effect.

# cold chocolate sauce

Made with cocoa powder and melted dark chocolate, this sauce is super chocolaty but quite a bit less rich than our hot fudge—and more satisfying on a warm day. Serve it at room temperature or chilled. For a thinner, more syrupy kind of sauce, increase the water by ½ cup.

*MAKES ABOUT 2½ CUPS*

½ cup unsweetened cocoa powder, sifted

1½ cups water

¾ cup sugar

¼ cup Corn Syrup Substitute (page 51)

8 ounces 70% dark chocolate, finely chopped (about 1 cup)

Pinch of kosher salt

1 teaspoon vanilla extract

Put the cocoa powder into a medium bowl and set aside. Put the water, sugar, and corn syrup substitute into a small, heavy-bottomed saucepan and bring to a boil over medium heat, whisking to dissolve the sugar. Add ½ cup of the hot syrup to the cocoa and whisk to make a completely smooth paste. Add the remaining syrup to the paste and whisk until smooth. Add the chocolate and salt and whisk until all the chocolate is melted. Whisk in the vanilla extract. Let the sauce cool at room temperature and store in an airtight container in the refrigerator for up to three weeks.

# raspberry coulis

"Coulis" is just a fancy word for a smooth sauce, and a simple raspberry coulis makes a great topping. Be sure to use raspberries when they are in season in your neck of the woods. If you can't find raspberries, you can substitute other berries like blackberries or strawberries. Frozen raspberries will do the trick in a pinch, but make sure they are completely thawed before using, and be aware that you may have to adjust the sugar to taste.

*MAKES ABOUT 2½ CUPS*

2 cups fresh or frozen raspberries (if using frozen, completely thawed)

¾ cup sugar

1 tablespoon freshly squeezed lemon juice

Put all the ingredients into a blender. Purée thoroughly, 30 to 45 seconds. Strain the purée through a fine mesh sieve. Discard the sieve contents. Serve cold. The coulis will keep, refrigerated, for up to 1 week.

# butterscotch sauce

Butterscotch sauce is a simple summer classic that's just too good! Use quality scotch in this recipe if you can, because its flavor plays a big role in the end. Something aged in oak for around 12 years would be ideal, like Singleton of Glendullan. Pair your butterscotch sauce with a scoop of Cappuccino or Vanilla Bean ice creams.

*MAKES 2½ CUPS*

½ cup (1 stick) unsalted butter

2 cups packed light brown sugar

1¾ cups heavy cream

1½ teaspoons salt

2 teaspoons vanilla extract

2 tablespoons single-malt scotch

In a medium, heavy-bottomed saucepan, melt the butter over medium-low heat. When the butter has melted, stir in the brown sugar using a wooden spoon. Continue cooking and stirring until the sugar does not appear grainy but looks thick and smooth, 8 to 10 minutes. Remove from the heat. Slowly and carefully whisk in the cream. Return to medium-low heat and let simmer for another 5 minutes, whisking occasionally. Remove from the heat and whisk in the salt.

Transfer the mixture to a large glass or metal bowl and let cool at room temperature for 30 minutes. Whisk in the vanilla and scotch. The butterscotch sauce can be served warm or at room temperature and will keep in an airtight container in the refrigerator for about one month.

# grilled stone fruit

As a kid from Idaho, I was always taught to get as much use out of a fire as you could. In honor of frontier-style resourcefulness, use the hot coals left over from your summer barbecue to grill up a few peaches, plums, or pluots, and pair them with Vanilla Bean Ice Cream. Simply delicious!

*MAKES 8 SERVINGS*

4 not-so-ripe stone fruits, cut into thick slices or just halved

Olive oil

Honey

Vanilla Bean Ice Cream (page 104)

Brush the fruit slices or halves with a light coating of olive oil. Place the fruit on the grill, cut side down. Grill until the surfaces have nice grill marks, about 5 minutes. Turn the fruit over, drizzle with honey, and grill for another 2 to 3 minutes. Serve in individual dishes topped with a scoop of Vanilla Bean Ice Cream.

# crispy nut cobbler-top crumble

Not feeling like baking a pie to go with your ice cream? No problem—we've got you covered with this tasty topping. Turn your favorite flavor of ice cream or sorbet into an à la mode treat by sprinkling this crumble over the top, or add it *and* a dollop of fruit compote for the ultimate deconstructed pie and ice cream dessert.

*MAKES ABOUT 2½ CUPS*

1 cup all-purpose flour

½ cup packed brown sugar

¼ cup granulated sugar

½ teaspoon kosher salt

½ cup almonds, pecans, walnuts, or hazelnuts (optional)

½ cup (1 stick) unsalted butter, chilled and cut into small pieces

Preheat the oven to 350°F. Line a baking sheet with parchment paper or a silicone baking mat. In a medium bowl, combine the flour, sugars, salt, and nuts. Add the butter and work it into the dry ingredients with your hands. The mixture should be clumpy, but with the butter pieces mostly incorporated. Distribute the crumble pieces evenly on the baking sheet. Bake for about 20 minutes, tossing and stirring every 6 or 7 minutes to prevent burning, until golden brown and evenly toasted. Remove from the oven and let cool.

Serve warm or at room temperature. The crumble can be stored in an airtight container at room temperature for about 2 weeks.

# corn syrup substitute

This syrup will work as a substitute in most recipes that call for corn syrup. (The exception is certain kinds of candy making. Although this syrup is practically identical to corn syrup in texture and taste, it does not have the same molecular structure, so it may not be appropriate to use in some more advanced candy-making recipes.) Be sure to have all the equipment you need for this recipe ready to go. After you have started to cook the sugar, you won't have time to be searching for anything.

*MAKES ABOUT 4 CUPS*

1³/4 cups water

4 cups sugar

¹/2 teaspoon cream of tartar

¹/4 teaspoon salt

Have a shallow stainless steel or tempered glass container at the ready for the cooked syrup. In a medium, heavy-bottomed saucepan fitted with a candy thermometer, add all the ingredients in order: first the water, then the sugar, the cream of tartar, and the salt. Bring to a boil over high heat and do not stir. While the sugar is cooking, use a pastry brush dipped in water to carefully brush off and discard any crystallized sugar that forms on the sides of the pot. Cook the mixture until it reaches 234°F on a candy thermometer, just prior to the soft-ball stage (see note).

Working quickly and carefully, remove from the heat and pour the hot liquid into the shallow container. Let cool to room temperature. Once cool, cover securely with plastic wrap, or pour it into a clean, odor-free plastic container with an airtight lid. Stored in a cool, dry place, this corn syrup substitute will keep for up to a year.

**NOTE**

*The sugar should be cooked to 235°F. Because hot sugar has a tendency to continue cooking after it has been removed from the heat source, removing it from the heat at 234°F helps ensure that it does not overcook.*

# fall

pumpkin clove ice cream

cinnamon ice cream

maple walnut ice cream

baracky road ice cream

cheese ice cream

fig ice cream

pear sorbet

cranberry sorbet

spiced cider sorbet

apple pie topping

pepita brittle

vanilla bean caramel

candied hazelnuts

# pumpkin clove ice cream

We get organic pumpkin purée from southern Oregon just before Halloween and keep this popular fall flavor on the menu through Thanksgiving. Make (or buy) a graham cracker crust, then fill it with this favorite for a homemade ice cream pumpkin pie. Drizzle the top with hot fudge, and you'll be the most popular person at the potluck!

*MAKES 1 TO 1½ QUARTS*

2 cups heavy cream

1 cup whole milk

1 cup sugar

Pinch of kosher salt

½ teaspoon ground cinnamon

½ teaspoon ground cloves

¼ teaspoon ground nutmeg

¾ cup pumpkin purée

1 teaspoon vanilla extract

Put the cream, milk, sugar, salt, cinnamon, cloves, and nutmeg into a small, heavy-bottomed saucepan and cook, uncovered, over medium-low heat, whisking occasionally to dissolve the sugar. Just before the mixture comes to a boil, remove from the heat. Pour the mixture into a shallow pan or bowl and whisk in the pumpkin purée. Place the mixture in the refrigerator to chill thoroughly, 1 to 2 hours.

When the mixture is cold, stir in the vanilla. Pour into an ice cream maker and process according to the manufacturer's instructions. Using a rubber spatula, transfer the ice cream to an airtight glass or plastic freezer container. Cover tightly and freeze until the ice cream is firm, at least 4 hours.

# cinnamon ice cream

Different kinds of cinnamon pack very different punches. For our cinnamon ice cream, we use an organic version of your everyday cinnamon, but there are other, more pungent types of cinnamon if you want to experiment and find which kind you like best (see note). Our cinnamon ice cream is a *huge* seller around the holidays and pairs well with almost every pie you can think of.

*MAKES 1 TO 1½ QUARTS*

2 cups heavy cream

1 cup whole milk

¾ cup sugar

Pinch of kosher salt

2½ teaspoons ground cinnamon (see note)

**NOTE**

*If you are looking to play around with different types of cinnamon, we recommend heading to World Spice Merchants at www.worldspice .com. Physically located near the Pike Place Market in Seattle, they are a favorite among home cooks and professionals alike. If you want to substitute Vietnamese or Chinese cinnamon, which are much more rich, sweet, and strong than conventional cinnamon, we recommend using only 1¾ teaspoons in this recipe.*

Put all the ingredients into a small, heavy-bottomed saucepan and cook over medium heat, whisking occasionally to dissolve the sugar and incorporate the cinnamon. Just before the mixture comes to a boil, remove from the heat. Pour the mixture into a shallow pan or bowl and place in the refrigerator to chill thoroughly, 1 to 2 hours.

When the mixture is cold, pour it into an ice cream maker and process according to the manufacturer's instructions. Using a rubber spatula, transfer the ice cream to an airtight glass or plastic freezer container. Cover tightly and freeze until the ice cream is firm, at least 4 hours.

# maple walnut ice cream

Maple walnut ice cream is a very old flavor that both Americans and Canadians claim as their own. This classic treat is sure to trigger nostalgia for anyone at your dinner table who is old enough to remember having a Victory Garden.

*MAKES 1 TO 1½ QUARTS*

2 cups heavy cream

1 cup whole milk

2 tablespoons sugar

Pinch of kosher salt

1 cup dark amber (grade A)
    maple syrup, chilled

1 teaspoon vanilla extract

1 teaspoon maple extract

1 cup coarsely chopped walnuts

Combine all the ingredients except the walnuts in a large bowl. Whisk until the sugar is completely dissolved. Pour it into an ice cream maker and process according to the manufacturer's instructions. During the last few minutes of processing, add the walnuts. Using a rubber spatula, transfer the ice cream to an airtight glass or plastic freezer container. Cover tightly and freeze until the ice cream is firm, at least 4 hours.

# baracky road ice cream

During the 2008 presidential election season, we had a little fun with serious matters and came up with a local hazelnut-based version of a classic. It was a sell-out flavor on November 4th! Hazelnuts grow well in Washington State, and we get ours from Holmquist Hazelnut Orchards in Lynden, Washington. Buy marshmallows or make your own to complete this traditional favorite.

*MAKES 1 TO 1½ QUARTS*

11 ounces 70% dark chocolate, coarsely chopped (about 1⅓ cups), divided

2 cups heavy cream

1 cup whole milk

¾ cup sugar

Pinch of kosher salt

1 teaspoon vanilla extract

¾ cup blanched, skinned, coarsely chopped hazelnuts

1 cup miniature marshmallows (see page 60)

Place 7 ounces (about 1 cup) of the chocolate in a medium bowl and set aside. Put the cream, milk, sugar, and salt into a small heavy-bottomed saucepan and cook uncovered, over medium heat, whisking occasionally to dissolve the sugar. Just before the mixture comes to a boil, remove from the heat. Pour the hot mixture over the chocolate and let sit for 5 minutes at room temperature. Whisk until the hot cream and chocolate are completely combined. Pour the mixture into a shallow pan or bowl and place in the refrigerator to chill completely, 1 to 2 hours.

When the mixture is cold, whisk in the vanilla. Pour into an ice cream maker and process according to the manufacturer's instructions. During the last minute of processing, add the hazelnuts, the remaining 4 ounces of chocolate, and the marshmallows. Using a rubber spatula, transfer the ice cream to an airtight glass or plastic freezer container. Cover tightly and freeze until the ice cream is firm, at least 4 hours.

# fig ice cream

Surprisingly enough, there are a handful of fig varieties that love the cool, wet Pacific Northwest climate. Black Mission figs from California are also readily available, and figs also grow well in Arkansas, Louisiana, Georgia, Texas, and South Carolina. Regardless of the type you choose, make sure your figs are ripe and that they taste sweet on their own before using them in this recipe. Try a scoop with some blue cheese crumbles and a drizzle of honey.

*MAKES 1 TO 1½ QUARTS*

12 ounces black figs (10 to 13 small), stems trimmed, quartered

½ cup plus ⅓ cup sugar, divided

2 cups heavy cream

1 cup whole milk

Pinch of kosher salt

1 teaspoon vanilla extract

Put the figs and ⅓ cup of the sugar into a small, nonreactive saucepan and cook over medium-low heat, stirring occasionally, to break down the figs to a jam-like consistency, about 10 minutes. Transfer the figs to a large bowl and place in the refrigerator to chill.

In another small saucepan, combine the cream, milk, remaining ½ cup sugar, and salt. Cook over medium heat, whisking constantly until the sugar is dissolved. Pour the mixture into a shallow pan or bowl and place in the refrigerator to chill thoroughly, 1 to 2 hours.

When both the fig and dairy mixtures are cold, combine them and whisk in the vanilla. Pour the mixture into an ice cream maker and process according to the manufacturer's instructions. Using a rubber spatula, transfer the ice cream to an airtight glass or plastic freezer container. Cover tightly and freeze until the ice cream is firm, at least 4 hours.

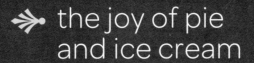

# the joy of pie and ice cream

What's a piece of pie without a scoop of ice cream? Really only half the fun, we say! Try one of our suggestions for pie and ice cream pairings to make your next holiday twice as tasty!

- Apple Pie and Cheese Ice Cream

- Cherry Pie and Meyer Lemon Ice Cream

- Chocolate Silk Pie and Salted Caramel Ice Cream

- Pecan Pie and Maple Walnut Ice Cream

- Peach Pie and Vanilla Bean Ice Cream

- Pumpkin Pie and Ginger Ice Cream

- Lemon Meringue Pie and Honey Lavender Ice Cream

- Banana Cream Pie and Melted Chocolate Ice Cream

- Summer Berry Pie and Lemon Verbena Ice Cream

- Chocolate Hazelnut Pie and Cappuccino Ice Cream

# pear sorbet

Another one of Christina's favorite sorbets! We like to use organic Bartlett pears from Oregon, because they are extra sweet, juicy, and soft when ripe. They also have thin and flavorful skin that adds color and texture to the final product. If you would prefer a smoother texture, strain the liquid through a fine mesh sieve before pouring it into your ice cream machine. Find a pear local to your area that you love on its own. Try a scoop of pear sorbet paired with a drizzle of Port Reduction (page 101).

*MAKES 1 TO 1½ QUARTS*

1½ cups sugar

1 cup water

3 ripe Bartlett pears, cored and quartered

1 tablespoon freshly squeezed lemon juice

Combine the sugar and water in a small, heavy-bottomed saucepan. Cook over medium heat, whisking occasionally, until the sugar is dissolved. Before the mixture comes to a boil, remove from the heat. Pour the mixture into a shallow pan or bowl and place in the refrigerator to chill completely, 1 to 2 hours. Meanwhile, in a blender, thoroughly purée the pears and lemon juice, 30 to 45 seconds. Place in the refrigerator to chill.

When the sugar syrup is cold, whisk in the pear purée. Pour the mixture into an ice cream maker and process according to the manufacturer's instructions. Using a rubber spatula, transfer the sorbet to an airtight glass or plastic freezer container. Cover tightly and freeze until the sorbet is firm, at least 4 hours.

# cranberry sorbet

Cranberries don't grow just anywhere, but lucky for us, the cold and wet of the Pacific Northwest is just perfect for them. I love this sorbet after any meal in late fall and winter. It makes a random Tuesday night feel like a holiday! Try drizzling a bit of hot fudge or cold chocolate sauce over a scoop for the ultimate flavor explosion.

*MAKES 1 TO 1½ QUARTS*

1¾ cups sugar

1 cup water

2½ cups fresh or frozen cranberries

1 tablespoon freshly squeezed lemon juice

Combine the sugar, water, and cranberries in a small, nonreactive saucepan and cook, uncovered, over medium high heat, whisking to dissolve the sugar. When the mixture reaches a boil, reduce the heat to medium and simmer until the cranberry skins rupture, about 5 minutes. Remove from the heat. Carefully pour the hot mixture into a blender and purée thoroughly, 30 to 45 seconds. Pour the mixture into a shallow pan or bowl and refrigerate until completely chilled, 1 to 2 hours.

When the mixture is cold, whisk in the lemon juice. Pour it into an ice cream maker and process according to the manufacturer's instructions. Using a rubber spatula, transfer the sorbet to an airtight glass or plastic freezer container. Cover tightly and freeze until the sorbet is firm, at least 4 hours.

# *spiced cider sorbet*

For this recipe, any cider will do. We once used a pint of apple-pear cider from the Columbia Gorge here in Washington, and it turned out to be our best batch. Find out what ciders your local orchards are making and try this recipe for a fresh fall flavor. Pair a scoop of this sorbet with a scoop of Salted Caramel Ice Cream for a twist on a caramel apple treat!

*MAKES 1 TO 1½ QUARTS*

2 cups sugar

1 cup water

1¼ teaspoons ground cinnamon

2 cups apple cider or juice

2 tablespoons freshly
squeezed lemon juice

Combine the sugar, water, and cinnamon in a small, heavy-bottomed saucepan. Over medium heat, bring just to a boil, whisking to dissolve the sugar. Pour the mixture into a large, shallow pan or bowl. Whisk in the apple cider and lemon juice. Place in the refrigerator to chill thoroughly, 1 to 2 hours.

When the mixture is cold, pour it into an ice cream maker and process according to the manufacturer's instructions. Using a rubber spatula, transfer the sorbet to an airtight glass or plastic freezer container. Cover tightly and freeze until the sorbet is firm, at least 4 hours.

# apple pie topping

This recipe is a favorite among Molly Moon's employees, especially when paired with apple compote atop Cinnamon Ice Cream. We put that combo on the menu, called it the "Just Like Apple Pie Sundae," and scoopers and customers couldn't get enough.

*MAKES ABOUT 3 CUPS*

1¼ cups all-purpose flour

¼ teaspoon kosher salt

¼ cup sugar

½ cup (1 stick) unsalted butter, chilled and cut into small pieces

¼ cup cold water

Preheat the oven to 325°F. Line a baking sheet with parchment paper or a silicone baking mat and set aside. Add the flour, salt, and sugar to the bowl of a food processor fitted with the blade attachment. Pulse briefly just to combine. Add the butter and pulse again briefly. The butter should still be in very small chunks, but evenly dispersed throughout the dry ingredients. Next, while pulsing, sprinkle in the water; the mixture will appear lumpy and be slightly sticky to the touch.

Spread the mixture evenly onto the baking sheet. Bake until light golden brown, 15 to 20 minutes, rotating the baking sheet halfway through the process. Serve warm or at room temperature. Store in an airtight container in the refrigerator for up to 2 weeks.

# pepita brittle

This brittle is my favorite of all kinds of brittle—and there are so many! I loved the taste of roasted pumpkin seeds from the Halloween pumpkin as a kid, and now we make this more adult pumpkin seed concoction to pair with fall sundaes. A jagged piece of this brittle makes a sophisticated accessory to a scoop of almost anything!

*MAKES ABOUT 2 CUPS*

1 cup pumpkin seeds

Large pinch of kosher salt

¼ teaspoon baking soda

1 cup sugar

¼ cup (½ stick) unsalted butter

¼ cup water

⅛ teaspoon freshly squeezed lemon juice

In a small bowl, toss together the pumpkin seeds, salt, and baking soda. Set aside. Line a baking sheet with a silicone baking mat or a piece of greased parchment paper and set aside.

Put the sugar, butter, water, and lemon juice into a medium, heavy-bottomed saucepan. Begin cooking over high heat, stirring just once or twice before the mixture comes to a boil. Let boil until the sugar begins to turn a medium amber color, at least 10 minutes.

Remove from the heat and quickly but carefully stir in the pumpkin seed mixture with a wooden or metal spoon. Use caution here, as the pumpkin seeds will pop and crackle slightly. Acting swiftly so as not to let the brittle cool in the pot, pour the contents out onto the baking sheet. While the brittle is still hot, flatten it slightly using the back of a spoon or a spatula sprayed with vegetable oil. Let the brittle cool completely at room temperature before handling. When completely cooled, break into bite-size pieces. Store in an airtight container for up to 1 week.

# vanilla bean caramel

This is a staple topping in the shops and has been since opening day. Served warm or cold, atop vanilla or chocolate, this recipe is one to master. Please note that making caramel is serious business, and it is imperative to pay the utmost attention at all times.

*MAKES ABOUT 2½ CUPS*

2 cups sugar

¼ cup (½ stick) unsalted butter

1¼ cups heavy cream

1 vanilla bean, split lengthwise

Pinch of kosher salt

**NOTE**

*Using a candy thermometer for this recipe is a must.*

Put the sugar into a small, heavy-bottomed saucepan. Over medium-high heat, slowly melt and caramelize the sugar, stirring occasionally with a wooden spoon, until it has completely dissolved and turned a golden amber color and reaches 330°F on a candy thermometer (see note), 12 to 15 minutes. Using a whisk, carefully mix in the butter. When the butter is melted and combined, remove the caramel from the heat and very gradually whisk in the cream. Be careful: the caramel will bubble up and steam significantly. When all the cream is incorporated, scrape the vanilla beans out of the vanilla pod and into the caramel, using a spoon or the back of a knife. Thoroughly whisk the beans into the caramel. Serve warm or at room temperature. Store in an airtight container in the refrigerator for up to 1 month.

# candied hazelnuts

This recipe is very versatile—you can use it to candy any kind of nut you like. We like to use hazelnuts, because they grow in the Pacific Northwest. Nuts are full of healthy fat, so be sure to keep a close eye on them while they are in the oven—they can burn easily.

*MAKES 4 CUPS*

4 cups hazelnuts, skins removed

¼ cup boiling hot water

1 cup sugar, divided

1 teaspoon of kosher salt

Preheat the oven to 325°F. Line a baking sheet with a silicone mat or greased parchment paper and set aside. Whisk ½ cup of the sugar into the hot water until the sugar is mostly dissolved. Put the hazelnuts into a large bowl and drizzle the sugar syrup over the top. Toss gently to coat. Using your hands or a slotted spoon, transfer the coated hazelnuts to another large bowl, leaving any leftover sugar syrup in the bottom of the first bowl. Sprinkle the remaining ½ cup sugar and the salt over the wet hazelnuts and toss to coat. Pour the nuts onto the prepared baking sheet and bake, tossing occasionally, until golden, about 20 minutes.

Remove the nuts from the oven and let cool completely on the baking sheet before handling. Once cooled, break up the nut clusters and store in an airtight container in a dry place for up to 3 weeks.

# winter

cardamom ice cream

meyer lemon ice cream

maple bacon ice cream

mexican chocolate ice cream

olive oil and toasted pine nut ice cream

chocolate coconut milk ice cream

kiwi sorbet

meyer lemon sorbet

mulled wine sorbet

blood orange sorbet

spiked whipped cream

spiced honey

deep, dark hot fudge

blood orange marmalade

port reduction

# cardamom ice cream

There is something about this spice that makes the texture of the ice cream just perfect. This is a flavor I first experienced at the Big Dipper in Missoula, Montana. We used to make gallons and gallons for an Indian restaurant on our block. It's now a winter staple at Molly Moon's.

*MAKES 1 TO 1½ QUARTS*

2 cups heavy cream

1 cup whole milk

¾ cup sugar

Pinch of kosher salt

1 teaspoon ground cardamom

Put all the ingredients into a small, heavy-bottomed saucepan with a lid and cook, uncovered, over medium heat, whisking occasionally to dissolve the sugar. Just before the mixture comes to a boil, remove from the heat. Cover and let the mixture steep at room temperature for 20 minutes. Pour the mixture into a shallow pan or bowl and place in the refrigerator to chill completely, 1 to 2 hours.

When the mixture is cold, pour it into an ice cream maker and process according to the manufacturer's instructions. Using a rubber spatula, transfer the ice cream to an airtight glass or plastic freezer container. Cover tightly and freeze until the ice cream is firm, at least 4 hours.

## best winter breakfast ever!

Ice cream is good on just about anything, but it is a particularly fun incentive for getting little ones to eat oatmeal on chilly winter mornings. You're already adding milk and sugar, so why not let the kiddos have what they really want for breakfast? Ice cream! At Molly Moon's, every year on the first Saturday in February we celebrate International Eat Ice Cream for Breakfast Day with oatmeal, ice cream, and an organic toppings bar that astounds our guests. Invite the neighbors over, and make a tradition of this fun holiday in your home!

# meyer lemon ice cream

This is another one of my favorites! Meyer lemons taste like a cross between a mandarin orange and a lemon. The scent and flavor are unique, and they're much sweeter than a conventional lemons. They are available for only a few months out of the year, and unfortunately they don't grow in the Pacific Northwest. But luckily the Lemon Ladies Orchard in Emerald Hills, in Northern California, has plenty. To order a box of your own, visit www.lemonladies.com.

*MAKES 1 TO 1½ QUARTS*

2 cups heavy cream

1 cup whole milk

¾ cup sugar

Pinch of kosher salt

4 tablespoons Meyer lemon zest (from about 3 lemons)

Combine the cream, milk, sugar, and salt in a small nonreactive saucepan with a lid. Cook, uncovered, over medium heat, whisking occasionally to dissolve the sugar. Bring to a simmer then remove from heat. Whisk in the lemon zest, cover, and let steep for 30 minutes at room temperature. Divide the cooled mixture in half and strain one half through a fine mesh sieve. Discard the sieve contents. Pour the strained mixture back into the unstrained mixture. Pour into a shallow pan or bowl and place in the refrigerator to chill thoroughly, 1 to 2 hours.

When the mixture is cold, pour it into an ice cream maker and process according to the manufacturer's instructions. Using a rubber spatula, transfer the ice cream to an airtight glass or plastic freezer container. Cover tightly and freeze until the ice cream is firm, at least 4 hours.

# mexican chocolate ice cream

Every year around Valentine's Day we like to spice things up a little with this variation of our favorite chocolate ice cream. Take a delicious chocolate ice cream recipe, add a dash of pungent Vietnamese cinnamon, and there you have it! If you can't find Vietnamese cinnamon, Chinese cinnamon will also do the trick. Indonesian cinnamon (the kind usually sold at the grocery store) is less spicy, but will still bring a warm kick of flavor.

*MAKES 1 TO 1½ QUARTS*

2 cups heavy cream

1 cup whole milk

2 tablespoons sugar

¼ teaspoon kosher salt

1 cup dark amber (grade A)
   maple syrup

1 teaspoon vanilla extract

1 teaspoon maple extract

1½ cups candied bacon
   pieces (page 83)

Place the chocolate in a medium bowl and set aside. Combine the cream, milk, sugar, salt, and cinnamon in a small, heavy-bottomed saucepan. Cook over medium heat, whisking occasionally to dissolve the sugar. When all of the sugar is dissolved and just before the mixture begins to boil, remove the saucepan from the heat. Pour the hot mixture over the chocolate and let sit for 5 minutes at room temperature. Whisk until the hot cream and chocolate are completely combined and no specks of chocolate remain. Place in the refrigerator to chill thoroughly, about 1 hour.

When the mixture is cold, whisk in the vanilla. Pour the mixture into an ice cream maker and process according to the manufacturer's instructions. Using a rubber spatula, transfer the ice cream to an airtight glass or plastic freezer container. Cover tightly and freeze until the ice cream is firm, at least 4 hours.

## make it spicy!

Add even more spice to our Mexican Chocolate Ice Cream by incorporating some real heat with dried chili peppers. There are countless varieties and combinations of chilies that could work fabulously in this recipe, but our favorites are the chipotle and the Pasilla de Oaxaca. The smokiness of the chipotle and the fruitiness of the Pasilla de Oaxaca really complement the sweet chocolate and creamy dairy. The standard caution applies: wear protective gloves and thoroughly wash your hands after working with the chilies. For this recipe, we suggest whisking in ¼ teaspoon of your preferred ground chili after all the ingredients have been combined, then slowly incorporating more, ¼ teaspoon at a time, tasting as you go, until the mixture reaches your desired spiciness. Keep in mind that the ice cream will get spicier as it sets in the freezer.

# mulled wine sorbet

Here in Washington we are lucky to have some great grape-growing weather. The best batch I've made of this sorbet was from a Zinfandel recommended by my friend Matti, who is a super taster. I bought a few bottles that he suggested, and one batch was just amazing! Since then, I've been referring to that special batch as "Matti's Mulled Wine Sorbet," but as things can go in a kitchen full of activity and wine, I can't, for the life of me, remember which bottle I used! Try your favorite Zinfandel, Cabernet, Demi Beaujolais, or Bordeaux and see what happens. This is a fun treat for a dinner party of wine buffs—see who can guess which wine was used!

*MAKES 1 TO 1½ QUARTS*

1 whole vanilla bean

2 cups sugar

3 cups red wine

1 cinnamon stick

5 whole cloves

1 orange, cut into six wedges

¼ teaspoon ground nutmeg

2 tablespoons finely chopped crystallized ginger

½ teaspoon whole allspice berries, or ¼ teaspoon ground allspice

Cut the vanilla bean in half lengthwise and, with the back of your knife, scrape out the seeds. Place both the seeds and the scraped pod in a medium, stainless steel saucepan with a lid. Add the remaining ingredients. Over medium heat, bring the mixture to a simmer, uncovered, whisking occasionally to dissolve the sugar. Reduce the heat to low and let gently simmer for 5 minutes. Remove from the heat, cover, and let steep for 30 minutes at room temperature. Strain the cooled mixture through a fine mesh sieve into a shallow bowl or pan. Discard the sieve contents. Place the mixture in the refrigerator to chill thoroughly, 1 to 2 hours.

When the mixture is cold, pour it into an ice cream maker and process according to the manufacturer's instructions. Using a rubber spatula, transfer the sorbet to an airtight glass or plastic freezer container. Cover tightly and freeze until the sorbet is firm, at least 4 hours.

# blood orange sorbet

The first batch of blood orange sorbet I ever made was based on a recipe posted on Shauna Ahern's blog, www.glutenfreegirl.com. It was an amazing, bright flavor to have kicking around my mouth in cold, wet January. This recipe is a bit simpler, but will still be the surprise you're looking for in that mid-winter slump!

*MAKES 3 TO 4 CUPS*

¼ cup water

1 cup sugar

2 cups blood orange juice
(from 6 to 8 oranges)

1 tablespoon freshly
squeezed lemon juice

Combine the water and sugar in a small heavy-bottomed saucepan. Over medium heat, bring just to a boil, whisking to dissolve the sugar, then remove from the heat. Whisk in the blood orange juice and lemon juice. Pour the mixture into a shallow pan or bowl and refrigerate until completely chilled, 1 to 2 hours.

When the mixture is cold, pour it into an ice cream maker and process according to the manufacturer's instructions. Using a rubber spatula, transfer the sorbet to an airtight glass or plastic freezer container. Cover tightly and freeze until the sorbet is firm, at least 4 hours.

# spiked whipped cream

Easy. Simple. Delicious. Need we say more?

*MAKES ABOUT 2½ CUPS*

1½ cups heavy cream

¼ cup confectioners' sugar, sifted

1 teaspoon vanilla extract

1 tablespoon Grand Marnier,
   Kirsch, or other liqueur

Using either a stand mixer fitted with a whisk attachment, a stainless steel bowl and a whisk, or a handheld electric mixer, beat the cream and sugar together until soft peaks form. Gradually sprinkle in the vanilla and liqueur and continue whisking until firm peaks form. Serve immediately.

# spiced honey

This recipe is so simple and useful that you might wonder why you didn't make it sooner. Be sure to use a mild honey so that the warm spices can take a turn pleasing your palate. Spiced honey is surprisingly good paired with a huge variety of ice creams—from melted chocolate to Meyer lemon to honey lavender. It's also perfect swirled into hot tea or, better yet, a hot toddy!

*MAKES ABOUT 2 CUPS*

2 cups honey

1 teaspoon ground cinnamon

½ teaspoon ground cardamom

½ teaspoon ground ginger

¼ teaspoon ground nutmeg

Pinch of kosher salt

1 tablespoon vanilla extract

Combine the honey, spices, and salt in a small saucepan. Cook gently over low heat, whisking occasionally. When the honey and spices have warmed through, remove from the heat. Transfer to a storage container and whisk in the vanilla extract. Serve warm or at room temperature. Spiced honey will keep indefinitely if stored in an airtight container in a cool, dry place. If it starts to crystallize, slowly heat it in the microwave or in a double boiler.

# deep, dark hot fudge

This classic topping is a staple in my fridge at all times. I am not embarrassed to say that many a breakfast in the last year has consisted of a banana dipped in hot fudge. I can really smother anything with this stuff. This extremely dark version of hot fudge perfectly complements our Salted Caramel Ice Cream (page 108).

*MAKES ABOUT 1 QUART*

1½ cups unsweetened
    cocoa powder

1½ cups sugar

½ teaspoon kosher salt

2 cups heavy cream

3 tablespoons unsalted butter

1½ teaspoons vanilla extract

Sift the cocoa powder, sugar, and salt together. Set aside. Combine the cream and butter in a medium, heavy-bottomed saucepan. Bring the cream barely to a simmer over medium heat, whisking occasionally to melt the butter. Reduce the heat to low. Gradually whisk the cocoa and sugar mixture into the hot cream, about ½ cup at a time, being sure to scrape the bottom of the pot with the whisk to prevent scorching. When all of the cocoa and sugar is thoroughly incorporated, remove from the heat. (If you like a thicker fudge, cook while whisking just a few minutes more on medium heat.)

Transfer the fudge to a storage container and allow it to cool slightly at room temperature, about 30 minutes. Whisk in the vanilla extract. Serve hot or warm. The fudge can keep for about 3 weeks, stored in an airtight container in the refrigerator. To serve on top of ice cream, reheat in the microwave or in a double boiler.

# blood orange marmalade

I love this topping on olive oil ice cream—and also on toast! It's like a grown-up version of Paddington Bear's comforting staple.

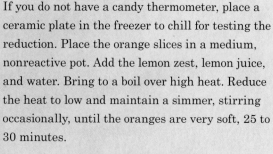

*MAKES ABOUT 2½ CUPS*

3 blood oranges (skin on), washed, cut into ⅛- to ¼-inch thick slices, seeded, and roughly chopped

1 tablespoon lemon zest

2 tablespoons freshly squeezed lemon juice

3 cups water

4 cups sugar

If you do not have a candy thermometer, place a ceramic plate in the freezer to chill for testing the reduction. Place the orange slices in a medium, nonreactive pot. Add the lemon zest, lemon juice, and water. Bring to a boil over high heat. Reduce the heat to low and maintain a simmer, stirring occasionally, until the oranges are very soft, 25 to 30 minutes.

Increase the heat and return to a full boil. Add the sugar, stirring the mixture continually until it darkens in color or reaches 222°F to 223°F on a candy thermometer, 20 to 25 minutes. Keep an eye on the heat, as the mixture may boil over.

To test the consistency of the marmalade, drop a small spoonful of the mixture onto the chilled plate and allow it to sit for 30 seconds. Then tilt the plate; if the mixture appears to be a soft gel that moves slightly, it is ready. If mixture is thin and runs easily, it needs to be cooked longer. When the marmalade has reached the correct consistency, remove from the heat and let sit at room temperature to cool, 45 minutes to 1 hour. Pour the marmalade into a glass or plastic storage container and store in the refrigerator for up to six months.

# *port reduction*

Port is a fortified wine traditionally from Portugal. Nowadays there are plenty of decent domestic producers of this fortified wine, and we encourage you to use your favorite for this recipe. We like to use ruby port just because it makes the color so gorgeous. For a sophisticated dessert, drizzle some on a scoop of pear sorbet.

*MAKES ABOUT 1¾ CUP*

3¼ cups ruby port

1 cup sugar

Put the port and sugar into a small, heavy-bottomed saucepan and bring to a boil over high heat, whisking to dissolve the sugar. Reduce the heat to low and let simmer until the mixture has reduced by half or until the temperature reads 225°F on a candy thermometer, 15 to 20 minutes.

Remove from the heat and let cool slightly at room temperature before pouring into a glass or plastic storage container. The reduction will thicken as it cools. Serve warm or at room temperature. Store in an airtight container in the refrigerator or at room temperature for up to 3 weeks.

# always

vanilla bean ice cream

melted chocolate ice cream

cappuccino ice cream

salted caramel ice cream

# vanilla bean ice cream

Most ice cream makers are judged by their version of vanilla. This simple flavor is one of the best—and quality, fresh ingredients make all the difference. Vanilla is one of the only ingredients in our shops that is not local, so we've made sure to taste test many, many kinds of organic, fair trade varieties. Experiment with the different vanillas available in your own neck of the woods!

*MAKES 1 TO 1½ QUARTS*

2 cups heavy cream

1 cup whole milk

3/4 cup sugar

Pinch of kosher salt

2 whole vanilla beans, split down the middle lengthwise

Combine all the ingredients in a small, heavy-bottomed saucepan and cook over medium heat, whisking occasionally. Just before the mixture comes to a boil, remove from the heat. Using tongs, carefully fish out the vanilla bean pods and, with the back of a knife, scrape the seeds into the pot. Put the scraped pods back into the pot and stir to combine. Pour the mixture into a shallow pan or bowl and place in the refrigerator to chill thoroughly, 1 to 2 hours.

When the mixture is completely chilled, remove the vanilla bean pods and discard. Pour the mixture into an ice cream maker and process according to the manufacturer's instructions. Using a rubber spatula, transfer the ice cream to a glass or plastic freezer container. Cover tightly and freeze until the ice cream is firm, at least 4 hours.

# melted chocolate ice cream

This recipe will forever change how you think about chocolate ice cream. We use Theo Chocolate Company's 70% dark chocolate in our ice cream at the shops. Theo's is an exemplary company, making organic and fair trade bean-to-bar chocolate and confections just a mile or so down the road from our Wallingford shop. They even give tours of their chocolate factory—a must for anyone visiting Seattle.

*MAKES 1 TO 1½ QUARTS*

7 ounces 70% dark chocolate, coarsely chopped (about 1 cup)

2 cups heavy cream

1 cup whole milk

3/4 cup sugar

Pinch of kosher salt

1 teaspoon vanilla extract

Place the chocolate in a medium bowl and set aside. Put the cream, milk, sugar, and salt into a small, heavy-bottomed saucepan and cook over medium heat, whisking occasionally to dissolve the sugar. Just before the mixture comes to a boil, remove from the heat. Pour the hot mixture over the chocolate and let sit for 5 minutes at room temperature. Whisk until the hot cream and chocolate are completely combined and no more flecks of chocolate can be seen. This may take quite a bit of whisking, but your determination will pay off in the smoothness of your final product. Pour the mixture into a shallow pan or bowl and place in the refrigerator to chill thoroughly, 1 to 2 hours.

When the mixture is cold, whisk in the vanilla. Pour into an ice cream maker and process according to the manufacturer's instructions. Using a rubber spatula, transfer the ice cream to a glass or plastic freezer container. Cover tightly and freeze until the ice cream is firm, at least 4 hours.

# cappuccino ice cream

As Seattleites, we are almost obligated to love good coffee. For most of my adult life, my apartment location priority has been anywhere within three blocks of the best coffee I could find in the city: Vivace Espresso. Their stand and shops have been my morning ritual, sometimes office, and hangout spot since 2002. I start almost every day with a cappuccino from my favorite baristas. This ice cream is a tribute to Don and Lisa, the best team at Vivace. It is the dessert version of the perfect cappuccino—8 ounces, double, sugar the shot, please!

*MAKES 1 TO 1½ QUARTS*

1 cup ground espresso beans

2½ cups heavy cream

1 cup whole milk

¾ cup sugar

Pinch of kosher salt

Thoroughly combine all the ingredients in an airtight container with a lid. Cover and refrigerate at least 12 hours or overnight. Strain the mixture through a fine mesh sieve, pressing to extract as much liquid as possible. Discard the sieve contents.

Pour the strained mixture into an ice cream maker and process according to the manufacturer's instructions. Using a rubber spatula, transfer the ice cream to a glass or plastic freezer container. Cover tightly and freeze until the ice cream is firm, at least 4 hours.

# salted caramel ice cream

This is the most popular flavor at Molly Moon's, by a *huge* margin. Don't be afraid of the salt. If the end product is too salty on its own, top this ice cream with hot fudge or serve it with a rich, dense brownie, and you'll be the happiest soul alive. My friend Linda has been serving our salted caramel ice cream on a brownie at her restaurant, Smith, in Seattle since 2008, making many fans of this combo. Be sure to make a very dark caramel—the intensity is necessary to balance out the complexity in this, our signature flavor. Because of the high salt content, the finished product will never be as firm as your other ice creams. This flavor is the softest ice cream we make. Be extra careful to chill everything before your ingredients go into the machine. Get this one into the freezer right away so it can set up as much as possible, and when you serve it, serve it fast!

*MAKES 1 TO 1½ QUARTS*

⅛ teaspoon freshly
   squeezed lemon juice

1½ cups sugar

1 tablespoon unsalted butter

3 cups heavy cream

1 cup whole milk

1 tablespoon kosher salt

**NOTE**

*In this recipe, the darker the caramel, the richer the flavor and the more balanced the salt will be. It is important to let the sugar caramelize to a dark amber hue before adding the butter. If you have a hood fan in your kitchen, this is a good time to use it, as making a darker caramel can sometimes get a little smoky. As with all caramel recipes, do not walk away from the stove, and be aware that the melted sugar is extremely hot.*

In a medium, heavy-bottomed saucepan over medium-high heat, add the lemon juice and then the sugar, ¼ cup at a time, stirring constantly with a wooden spoon. Wait to add each batch of sugar until the previous batch is completely dissolved. After all the sugar is added to the pot, continue to cook until it caramelizes to a dark golden brown, 4 to 6 minutes (see note). Switch to a whisk and carefully mix in the butter. After the butter is completely melted, reduce the heat to medium-low and very slowly whisk in the cream and milk, being extra careful, as the caramel will steam significantly. Remove from the heat. Pour the mixture into a shallow pan or bowl and place in the refrigerator to chill thoroughly, 1 to 2 hours.

When the mixture is cold, whisk in the salt, then pour into an ice cream maker and process according to the manufacturer's instructions. Using a rubber spatula, transfer the ice cream to a glass or plastic freezer container. Cover tightly and freeze until the ice cream is firm (it will not freeze very hard), at least 4 hours, but 24 hours is best.

# INDEX

Note: Photographs are indicated by *italics*.

# ABOUT THE AUTHORS

*molly moon neitzel* (left) is an expert ice cream eater turned enthusiastic ice cream maker. After an exciting career in the political and music industries, Neitzel gave in to her obsession for creamy, frozen deliciousness in the spring of 2008: aiming to give the people of Seattle what they were missing most, she opened her first Molly Moon's Homemade Ice Cream shop. Neitzel's five scoop shops and signature Molly Moon's blue ice cream truck have been recognized for bringing fun, locavore ice cream flavors to the Pacific Northwest. Molly Moon's has been hailed as one of the best ice cream brands in the United States by *Bon Appétit*, *Sunset*, *Food & Wine*, and *Travel + Leisure* magazines. Neitzel lives in Seattle with her lovable Frenchton pup, Parker Posey, and her even more lovable husband, Zack.

Following an environmental studies degree at the University of Washington and an adventure hiking the Pacific Crest Trail, *christina spittler* (right) dove into studying pastry at the Seattle Culinary Academy. Her environmental ethic, passion for all things edible, and culinary expertise led the Northern California native to the pastry kitchens at Seattle's Earth and Ocean and Rover's, and finally, to became head chef at Molly Moon's Homemade Ice Cream. Spittler is also the author of the humorous food blog *Be Coolinary*.